THE BUSINESS OWNER'S GUIDE TO

Choosing & Using a Solicitor

Bart Daly

corporate group

Published by Oak Tree Press, Cork T12 XY2N, Ireland.
www.oaktreepress.com / www.SuccessStore.com

© 2024 Bart Daly

Cover design: Kieran O'Connor Design.

A catalogue record for this book is available from the British Library.
ISBN 978-1-78119-660-1 Paperback
ISBN 978-1-78119-661-8 PDF
ISBN 978-1-78119-662-5 ePub

For EU product safety concerns, please contact Oak Tree Press at NSC Campus, Manhon, Cork T12 XY2N, Ireland or info@oaktreepress.com.

Contents

Preface

As the owner of a business, it is inevitable that at some stage you will need the services of a solicitor. Like every profession or trade, there are good solicitors and not so good ones. But to avoid ending up with the latter should not be left to good luck. This book is intended to help you as a business owner to make an informed choice in finding the best solicitor for your particular needs – although note that I have confined this book to engaging a solicitor for civil matters only, not criminal.

Different countries have different court systems, but legal professionals are the same the world over. Solicitors are trained and experienced at advising on a variety of legal matters and initiating or defending litigation. They are not magicians, so you should have realistic expectations of the outcome once the solicitor is engaged. Too often, solicitors are sought only after a problem has arisen, when the client has an expectation that the solicitor will 'sort it'.

The intervention of a solicitor can bring about a positive outcome or reduce the exposure you might otherwise have, but these are dependent on an entire range of factors. For this reason, a (good) solicitor will not make statements like 'We will win this case'. Instead, they can offer an opinion on whether your case is strong or weak, subject to a complete appraisal of the facts.

The book starts by explaining the services solicitors offer, how to choose a solicitor suited to your needs and the initial stage of first engagement. Next, we look at how you should work with your chosen solicitor to ensure that you get the best out of the relationship. Then, since so many legal situations end up in litigation in the courts, we consider the key issues here – including alternative dispute resolution, a way of resolving issues without recourse to the courts. And last, just in case, we reflect on what happens when things go wrong – as, sadly, they sometimes do.

I have been both a practicing barrister and a litigant, so I have experience from both sides. I was also a law publisher to the legal profession for over

30 years. I hope readers will find this book a useful guide to engaging the services of legal professionals. They are there to help you, so if you have a clear understanding of how solicitors work, this should remove any of the unknown factors and enable you to work with your solicitor for a common purpose and an optimum result.

The opinions expressed in this book are entirely my own.

Bart D. Daly, October 2024

Chapter 1

The Services Solicitors Provide

People often associate solicitors with litigation and indeed sometimes people's first contact with a solicitor is when they are being sued or want to sue. But the converse is the reality of solicitors' work.

The range of work is considerable and mostly non-contentious, such as property selling and buying, wills, divorce, contracts, immigration, and advisory work.

Those engaged in commercial life would benefit from lawyers' advice on:
- Setting up a new business.
- Employee rights and employee contracts.
- Sale and acquisition of assets.
- Commercial contracts and outsourcing.
- Environment issues.
- Health and safety issues.
- Fraud.
- Employee termination.
- Workplace accidents.
- Data protection.
- Product liability.
- Professional liability.
- Information technology issues.
- Crisis management.
- Tribunal representation.
- Agricultural matters.
- Legal taxation issues.
- … and more.

Many of the above can create legal issues which, if not managed properly, have the potential to incur financial loss, whereas preventive legal advice can avert trouble and save money.

The corporate sector has a considerable body of regulatory obligations to comply with so legal advice on preventing future problems arising makes sense.

Individuals too can avail of solicitors on an entire range of areas, such as:
- Disputes with neighbours.
- Wills.
- Divorce and marital problems.
- Children.
- Property.
- Adoption.
- Consumer rights.
- Personal injury.
- Workplace accidents.
- Road traffic accidents.
- Employment rights.
- Immigration.
- Defamation.
- Medical negligence.
- Data protection.
- Class actions.

… and more.

Note that the role of the barrister is quite different to that of the solicitor – see **Appendix 1.**

Choosing a Solicitor

In many ways, this is the most important chapter in this book. Most aspects of running a business in Ireland have government regulations. It is important that from the outset business owners are aware of these regulations and that they are compliant. The best way to ensure this is to have a solicitor whom you can trust and rely on when required.

A solicitor will advise on the areas you could have issues with and how to deal with them. But it normally doesn't work like that! Sadly, too many business owners' first contact with a solicitor occurs only after a problem arises.

So, a problem surfaces. For your company, it is important, and you need to get it resolved. You may have tried to resolve it yourself but failed and (unknowingly) possibly made things worse. Many proprietors of small businesses try to sort out disputes themselves or draft what they believe is a straightforward contract without legal advice. In some cases that is fine, but if they find themselves unable to do so and they then bring in a solicitor later, it may be too late to resolve the problem and so the solicitor's job becomes one of damage limitation.

An example of this is where an issue arises with an employee. Employment law is heavily regulated. It can be a minefield for the non-professional to cope with. Many internal employment issues are handled by the company without the advice of the company solicitor. This is a recipe for disaster. The Workplace Relations Commission has month on month cases where 'fair procedures' were not complied with in dealing with a problem with an employee. Fair procedures are a principle enshrined in law where an independent person must carry out an investigation into the disciplinary process. Failure to provide this could lead to high awards against the company and, for small companies, such awards could affect their existence.

By the time the solicitor comes on board, the damage is often done. Then the business owner is on the defensive and the cost of defending such cases has to be found. For small employers, when handling legal issues themselves on what appears to be straightforward cases, even with the best of intentions they can find that they have transgressed the law by some procedure or lack of procedure.

When two parties are contracting, they may put on paper what their respective roles are. At this time there is goodwill between the parties and eagerness to get on with the business. In some such situations, they may commit to paper the 'arrangement' between them. They might be friends or even related and may not feel the need for a formal contract. This is another recipe for disaster. People fall out. Then one of the parties goes to their solicitor, and guess what? One could drive tractors through the gaps in the contract. These situations can be extremely hard to solve and costly too.

So, you have a problem, and it needs sorting. You may have used a solicitor in the past. Do not automatically lift the phone to ring 'your' solicitor. First, ask yourself, *'Is this solicitor right for this problem?'*

You may know solicitors from a sporting club or socially and they are nice people. Sure they are, but do they have the right experience to take your problem on? A solicitor's work is to assist and resolve legal problems for their client, **but their skill also is in preventing legal problems**. The wisdom of engaging a solicitor to advise you on dealing with commercial issues surrounding the introduction of a new product or service could save your company a lot of money if any claims arise..

So how do you choose the right solicitor?

Horses for Courses

If you have a sore back and you know of a doctor who has a good reputation for bad backs do you go to him/her or to your own doctor and hope for the best? Well, the same applies to solicitors. Most law firms have a general practice, and their websites will tell you the areas of law they practice in. So, if you have a trademark problem and your usual solicitor's firm does not list this on its website among the services it provides, then that solicitor is not for you.

If you have a good relationship with a solicitor you have used in the past but believe that solicitor may not have the experience in your area of concern you could contact him/her and ask them to refer you to a solicitor with the expertise you need. This may be a good starting point but nonetheless, before following up on the name, still conduct your own research.

Before you ask around, do your own research. Google solicitors in your city or area with expertise in the area of law your problem is in. Ask people you know if they can recommend anyone. Ideally, find a solicitor whose office is geographically close to you for your convenience.

You can decide whether you want a big, medium, or small firm. The size of a firm does not necessarily mean it is better. The bigger ones will be more expensive, and they will have highly skilled solicitors employed. But there are many smaller firms with particular expertise and lower cost that are just as good. This latter type of firm is often referred to as a boutique firm.

When choosing a solicitor, it is wise to find one who has experience in the area of law of interest to you. So, if you want a specialist – that is a solicitor with a lot of experience in the area you require – then eliminate the firms that appear to have a general practice.

When you think you have found a solicitor that suits your needs or when you have drawn up a shortlist, ask around if people you know have used them and what they thought of them. Some firms on their websites have endorsements; these can be useful but do not take them as gospel, still do your own research. While this takes time, it will be worth it in the end.

While law firms' websites are informative, they are not objective, so you need to do your own homework. The more time you put into finding the solicitor for you the better chance of getting one suited to your business problem, so you start with a feeling of confidence in your choice of solicitor.

Fees

Ask around for what people paid for solicitors. This will give you a general 'feel' for this important matter. Look to see if their websites cover fees. Not all do but for those that do, this is useful information for you before initiating contact.

Bigger firms usually have an hourly rate so be sure to find out this information before engaging the solicitor.

The fees question is particularly important so do as much research as you can on this matter before meeting the solicitor. Fees can vary. The cheapest is not always the best option. At this stage, you are only getting ballpark figures, but it prepares you for the outlay you will incur and, although we'll consider legal fees in more detail in **Chapter 8**, it's good to have a real understanding of this before venturing further.

There is a difference between advisory work and litigation. In the former, the expertise is within the law firm so it is here you are paying the hourly rate and fees should be easier to estimate. For instance, a solicitor should know how long it will take in drafting a contract so should be able to quote a fee for their time. In litigation, solicitors acting for you will incur costs in issuing and serving the proceedings, so it is reasonable for them to seek some costs upfront for this. But they should be able to give a reliable estimate of this cost.

Where a barrister is being engaged (see **Appendix 1**), you need to find out what additional fees you will incur. Your point of contact is the solicitor you first engaged with and any contact with a barrister will be through the solicitor.

In litigation, surprises can occur adding time to the preparation of the case and making it harder to pin down the final cost, but your solicitor should inform you of this in advance and how it will add to the cost.

Do as much groundwork on these matters before contacting the solicitor you have chosen and then discuss your likely fee exposure.

Litigation Considerations

If the matter you are seeking advice on is contentious and litigation is likely, then remember the solicitor spends a good deal of their time in the local courts and thus will be harder to contact while out of the office. Certainly, the solicitor will research the matter, and consult the legislation and case law before forming an opinion on where your case is going.

Preferably discuss this with the solicitor at the first meeting. If the solicitor believes the case will be a 'fighter,' ask the solicitor, have they dealt with similar cases in the past? If so, how do they see your case panning out? The solicitor can only express their opinion as every case is different and contains different components, and while the case may be in the same area of law, there are so many permutations that the solicitor will not be able to predict the outcome but only offer their opinion based on their experience and based on the information you have supplied.

It is at this stage that the possibility of settlement can be discussed and when would be the best time to raise this with the other side. Whether your solicitor makes the first move or awaits an approach from the other side is a matter for them. Negotiation is a skill and needs to be dealt with in a strategic way. Before that is considered, your case's strengths and weaknesses must be assessed.

Do

- Conduct independent research on finding the right solicitor for you.
- Seek a solicitor who has experience in the area you need.
- Research law firms' websites to get an idea of the fees you could incur.

Don't

- Don't try to solve a legal issue yourself; seek help.
- Don't rush in engaging a solicitor; make your choice after careful research.

Chapter 3
First Contact with the Solicitor

Okay, so now you have done your due diligence and are about to contact the selected solicitor.

It is critically important that for this meeting you either take notes yourself or bring a good note-taker. These notes may be referred to a lot later on, and particularly if the relationship with your solicitor sours.

Before the meeting, open a file for the history of all correspondence that will be exchanged once the solicitor has been engaged. Retain a copy of all documentation you hand over to the solicitor. If they are original documents indicate them as such. There may be witnesses you need; contact them and ascertain if they are willing to give evidence. Gather names, addresses, mobile numbers, email addresses, dates of incidents, etc.

Make a checklist of all the issues you need to discuss with the solicitor. At the conclusion of the meeting, check the list to ensure you have covered all the points.

The first meeting is exploratory. You are there to ascertain for yourself that this solicitor is who you want. You will be weighing them up and they too will be weighing you up. First impressions are very important. Most first meetings or consultations are free but be sure to check this at the time of first contact. Don't be afraid to enquire if the solicitor has had cases similar to yours in the past and how much experience they have in the area.

Solicitors are human like the rest of us and come in diverse personalities. While as a group they tend to be conservative, some would be more conservative than others. This you will see from the initial meeting, and you need to decide whether you think you can work with this person. Will they be running your case or another solicitor in the firm? If the latter, you need to meet that person. Will your personalities work or clash?

Things to Watch Out For

Attentiveness
Is the solicitor a good listener, are they taking notes, are they punctual, have they devoted uninterrupted time to this consultation and not allowed the consultation to be disturbed with phone calls, texts, and emails? An exception to this would be a litigation solicitor, where their time often overruns with cases running late and so on, but this should be explained from the outset.

A Presumption that You Are Already a Client
If this is the case, you need to put the brakes on and remind them that this is an exploratory meeting.

Vagueness on Questions Asked
Not getting clear answers is a worrying signal. You must emerge from the meeting with a clear understanding of the issues raised.

Over-enthusiasm
Most solicitors are conservative so if you come across an over-eager one, beware.

If you ask the solicitor at the exploratory meeting what are your chances of success having outlined the case, most will be careful in their response; so, if you come across one who gives you the feeling it is an open and shut case, it's time to move on to the next name on your list. There are too many unknown factors in litigation to consider before predicting success. There is nothing wrong in saying you appear to have a good or strong case but so early in the process anything more is reckless and misleading.

Fees

Fees can be a thorny issue, so it is best to tackle it early to avoid any misunderstandings later. It would be good to state at the start that you have to budget for this so you need to know exactly what the costs will be and how they are structured. Many solicitors charge by the hour. Partners (the senior solicitors in a law firm) will charge more than assistant/junior solicitors. You need to know who is handling your case (it is not necessarily the person you meet at the introductory meeting). On being told the hourly rates you need to ask if one solicitor or more will be involved. If you get an answer like *'it is not envisaged more than one will be required'* you need to get clarification on this as that answer leaves the door open to another joining the team and your fees escalating. It is reasonable to enquire into the role of trainees, paralegals and if you are paying for them.

If the solicitor says they can only make a general estimate of the fees, this would be a concern; they should have a good idea of the fees, and this might need further probing. You need to know the fee exposure you will be incurring.

Normally upfront advances of fees should be avoided but in the current economic climate it may not be unreasonable if the sum sought is reasonable and in the form of a deposit.

Don't get too hung up on comparing hourly rates among law firms; a highly experienced specialist may charge a higher rate, but they are more likely to get the work done more quickly. The key point here is to get an estimate of how many hours the job will take.

If the notes taken at the explanatory meeting estimate the work is to be done in, say, fifty fee-paying hours and you get a bill for considerably more than that, you will have the notes of your exploratory meeting to dispute the increased fee. The solicitor will have to justify the significant increase in fee. With what had been decided at the initial meeting, unless the solicitor can show they alerted you to the increase in fees, they will have a difficult job in justifying the increase and even less chance of getting it.

When engagement of the solicitor has been agreed it can be useful to agree a staged payment of their fee. This is good for the solicitor but better for you as you will avoid a big bill at the conclusion of the work and will be able to stay on budget as the work progresses.

In litigation, if you are a plaintiff you need to be aware that if you lose the case, you may be paying both your costs and the other party's costs. In addition to fees, solicitors often charge for 'outlay' such as couriers, phone calls, photocopying, scanning, stamps, etc. so at this meeting ask about these items too. Some firms may cover these costs in their overhead, but it is another cost you need to know about.

At the conclusion of your exploratory meeting, you must feel confident that this solicitor will be competent to handle your work. You also need to be completely satisfied with the fee structure.

Statutory Obligations of Solicitors

There are regulations that regulate how their registered members' work. Your solicitor will inform you of any regulations you need to be aware of. Additionally, solicitors are obligated to send you a letter of engagement. This will set out the solicitor's terms and conditions of business and will request information from you to comply with anti-money laundering requirements.

Setting the Ground Rules

At this first meeting, enquire what the solicitor's practice is regarding communication with clients on cases. You will want to avoid weeks or months of no news so this needs to be clarified with your chosen solicitor at the outset. If this is agreed, then there will not be a need for endless phone calls seeking to know what is happening. Litigation has certain stages in processing the court documents so explaining the time scales for these should not be a problem.

Delays in litigation are not uncommon. There should be an agreed arrangement that phone calls or emails will be responded to in a pre-agreed time limit. There is nothing more frustrating than chasing up a solicitor who does not return phone calls.

You should also raise the query as to what will happen to your case if the solicitor gets involved in another, bigger, case. This happens, so there needs to be a contingency plan which will meet your needs and not leave your case less prioritised.

You should discuss at this meeting the question of a problem arising between you and your solicitor and what procedures they would recommend dealing with it. Hopefully, no problems will arise or if so, they can be cleared up quickly, and if you have a good relationship with your solicitor then it will be resolved. However, in the instance of a serious matter you could enquire whether they would be open to arbitration. Most good solicitors would not oppose this method. However, my experience is that legal professionals do not like others looking into how they run their business so if there is a resistance to arbitration, they need to have some acceptable procedure in place to deal with the complaint or breakdown in the working relationship. Many solicitors will have a Grievance Procedure on their website; you should read this.

So, any problems arising in the course of working with your solicitor can be resolved by an upfront exchange at the initial meeting and agreeing procedures to deal with any problems arising in the future. You do not want a falling-out with your solicitor, a stand-off with virtually no communication between you both and the hassle and additional cost of changing law firms.

Do

- Take notes and keep a record of all communications with the solicitor.
- Collect all documents.
- Retain a copy of all documents.
- Enquire whether the solicitor has done similar work.
- Discuss fees and methods of paying.

Don't

- Don't hold back documents or information.
- Don't take shortcuts in assembling the information.
- Don't judge your choice of solicitor on fees; the cheapest may not be the best.
- Don't leave the meeting with unanswered questions.

Chapter 4

Understanding the Client / Solicitor Relationship

At this juncture you have engaged a solicitor and have confidence in your selection. It is important to see the relationship between the two of you as being part of a team, with the solicitor being the project leader. He or she will lead the project and will seek to gather all the information that is needed.

It is important to understand the differing roles the parties play. The client will be, understandably, subjective whereas the solicitor must be objective in their work and approach. Solicitors are forensic in their pursuit of relevant information. They cannot proceed with the work until all the relevant information has been obtained. This pursuit of information requested by the solicitor may be a nuisance or inconvenience, but they are acting in your best interests and want to avoid any surprises that may surface at a critical time later.

When asked for a list of information that is needed, be sure to obtain it. Don't be judgemental and decide they won't need this or that. Let the solicitor decide what is relevant to your case.

Remember time is money – your money. If you assemble all the requested information together and bundle it in a folder for the solicitor and let them sort it out, it is wasting your money. Take the time to order the documents into sequential order. The solicitor is skilled at ascertaining the legal issues, separating the relevant facts from the irrelevant. The solicitor is not a filing clerk but, if you give them that chore you will be paying their normal hourly rate (expensive clerk!).

In assembling the requested information, do not be selective in deciding if this email or that letter is of use. Remember who is the project leader. It is their job to decide what stays in the file and what can be discarded.

Be careful with emails: do a search and print all the emails from the parties involved. Some email services bundle the emails together, so you need to painstakingly read them all so that none are excluded. It is a tedious task but sometimes a critically important detail is found in an innocent looking email.

Do not delete or destroy any document or email, even if you are certain that it contains nothing of interest. In litigation it is common to seek 'discovery orders' and if one is served on you for, say, email correspondence then you have to comply with the order. If the other side, during discovery, finds that an email was deleted (even though you believe it had no value) the court may take the view that evidence was destroyed. Your solicitor will walk you through any discovery procedure, but once legal proceedings are initiated, or indeed intended to be issued, destruction of any documents must be avoided. There are software programmes now that make email discovery easier, and your solicitor could advise you here.

In the early stages of litigation, you will see more of your solicitor as the information is gathered, and here your relationship should deepen as you get to understand each other's needs. If you feel issues are getting complex, ask questions so you stay on top. You, the client, need to be informed and understand what is happening. Solicitors tend to be quite literal in their manner so if you ask a question, be specific. Solicitors cannot read your mind, so be clear.

Your solicitor will distinguish between the points in your case – the strong ones and the weak. They may eliminate certain evidence which you may not agree with. They have their reasons but ask why; you need to know and cannot or should not be left in the dark.

It is fine to put your total trust in your solicitor, but this does not mean you abandon them to carry the case. You are an important part of the team so be informed and know and understand everything your solicitor is doing on your case – after all it is *your* case.

It is only natural that a client takes a case personally so emotions can run high at times. You may feel a certain line should be taken but your solicitor is reluctant to go with that. They have their reasons. Ask them why. It may be that a certain person may not make a good witness and under cross-examination could in fact harm your case. This is the solicitor acting in the overall best interests of your case. They are being objective and weighing up the pros and cons.

Looking at your case from the familiar surroundings of your office or home may give you confidence of success but on the day in court, witnesses are in the cold, unfriendly, almost clinical surroundings of a courtroom and this can unnerve them. Solicitors will, when meeting clients and potential witnesses, weigh up whether they think the person before them will be a good witness. This is down to their expertise and judgement. Having a good case on paper is one thing but that has to be delivered in court by oral evidence and if the solicitor has any doubt on this, they will take that into consideration on how best to win your case.

You, as the client, need to be rational at critical decision times. There is no room for taking umbrage or seeking revenge on the other party. This could distract from the matter at hand – winning the case. The case will be decided on the law, not on how one feels about the other party. Here the solicitor will steer you on the right path so be warned to put aside your hostile feelings for revenge. Also, you need to avoid getting on the wrong side of a judge.

You may have a good case, but good cases can be lost by a nervous witness and good solicitors can win bad cases. If you or one of your witnesses performs poorly in the witness box, the solicitor on the other side will be presented with an opportunity and you can be sure they will not pass on it. So, listening to your solicitor here is important. Their advice on how they will present your case in court is based on their expertise; this is their backyard, and this advice should be heeded, not resisted.

The time up to the day in court is all preparation. In the course of this period, issues will arise which may alter the intended plan. Documentary evidence may not stack up as hoped; there may be an inconclusive paper trail; a witness may be deceased or living abroad and you need to decide if it is worth the cost of bringing them back; or a former employee may have since gotten married, changed their name and become untraceable. Evidence of your case needs to be produced in court and it does not always pan out the way you first thought or hoped. Here you will see your solicitor at work, acting in your best interest. As the landscape of your case shifts the solicitor has to respond and chart out the best course for you with the evidence they have to work with.

Do

- Use the time with your solicitor wisely.
- Give the documents requested in sequential order.
- Trust the judgement of your solicitor.
- Ask questions if you don't understand anything.

Don't

- Don't destroy documents.
- Don't delete emails.
- Don't hide evidence.

Chapter 5
Working as a Team

Once you engage a solicitor to take on your case you are strengthening your team to achieve the result you want.

You do not 'hand over' the matter and leave it to the solicitor to solve. The papers and briefing you give the solicitor will inform them of the issues at hand but as the case progresses, they will need you to be involved. As a team player, withholding information from your solicitor of development at your end will not help and may, in fact, damage your case.

If you are concerned about an approach the solicitor is taking, discuss it with them. Do not let it fester to a point where it is too late to raise the issue or do anything with it. Your solicitor needs to know how you are feeling as progress is made. They will not be offended, or should not be offended, by asking questions on why they are recommending a particular course of action. There will be a reason why a solicitor is proceeding in a certain way, but you need to understand why and be comfortable with it.

Even if your solicitor is the best in their area, a client's input is coming from a different angle, and this can contribute to the outcome of the discussion. If your solicitor is a sole practitioner, this is even more reason for a second view on the issues.

By working with your solicitor, you will understand their personality and approach to issues. This of course could irritate you but at least you can understand how they approach things. It also gives you the opportunity to investigate with your solicitor whether it is the right approach. They will be coming to the problem objectively whereas you, the client, will be subjective and, at times, emotionally involved. Your solicitor needs to understand how you are approaching the issues, and this can only be understood by working together.

Communication with your solicitor is critical to achieve results.

Do

- Give facts.
- Be a team player.
- When relaying facts, clearly state these (not your opinion on the facts).
- Hand over all documentation.
- Organise the documentation in sequential order.
- Keep a record of all dealings with legal advisors.
- Keep a record and copies of everything handed over.

Don't

- Don't withhold information.
- Don't confuse facts with your opinion on facts.
- Don't keep your legal advisors in the dark about developments.
- Don't be untruthful.
- Don't expect miracles; be realistic in your expectations.

Chapter 6
Trust & Openness

Any relationship needs trust and openness on both sides to work. The client has a problem they cannot resolve themselves and their solicitor has the skill to assist with that problem. The solicitor, once engaged, is on your side.

Some people think that solicitors are too friendly with each other and become suspicious if they see their solicitor talking – or worse, laughing – with an opposing solicitor. Compared to other industries, the legal profession is quite small. In the same city or county, it is possible solicitors will know each from the law school or university they studied in. So, it is inevitable that, in such communities, solicitors will know each other.

Clients take cases personally, that is not unusual. They feel aggrieved at a contract that was broken or some injury or cost to them caused by another person or company. But the solicitor takes an objective perspective. Solicitor X may represent you and solicitor Y may represent the other party. Regardless of whether they know each other, they will put your case first and keep their acquaintances or friendship with the opposing solicitor. They are professionals and this will not influence their representation of your interests.

Both may be social or sporting friends. They could play a round of golf together and never mention your case. Why? Well, one reason is that they have at any one-time dozens of clients' cases at various stages of resolution but, most importantly, if you do not brief them to discuss the case informally with the other party, they will not. Trust. After all, they are probably on the golf course to get away from clients! A solicitor is not going to jeopardise their relationship with a client by doing solo runs without discussing it in advance with them. Conversely, a solicitor might ring their client and say they are matched to play golf with the opposing solicitor and ask the client shall they use the opportunity to raise their case and see what happens.

Solicitors act on the instructions of their clients. If they overstep that mark, then they are in breach of their instructions and should be dismissed. The client must be informed at all times of contact with the opposing party.

Remember trust goes both ways and solicitors act on information supplied to them. As the client, you need to ensure the information supplied is accurate. If you notice an error, you should inform the solicitor of the error. A client withholding information is not a good idea. A client may be embarrassed about some aspect and decide to 'hold back for the moment.' How can your solicitor advise you if you give incomplete information to them?

Withholding information may be innocent. A client may subjectively decide 'this is not important' and discard it. Let the solicitor be the judge of what is important and not important.

Once you have engaged a solicitor, do not contact the other party. Any communication by you to the other side must be done via your solicitor. To do otherwise is unhelpful to your case and a guaranteed way of falling out with your solicitor.

Do

- Trust your legal team to act in your best interests.
- Consider allowing your solicitor the opportunity to informally discuss your case with the opposing solicitor if they suggest it.

Don't

- Don't withhold any information from your legal team.
- Don't be suspicious if your solicitor is personal friends with the opposing party's solicitor.
- Don't communicate with the other party yourself.

Chapter 7

Agreements & Contract Negotiations

All significant commercial transactions, whether it is for the provision of services or the sale or acquisition of an asset, will require the deal to be reduced to paper.

The commercial parties may agree to do the deal 'subject to contract'; it is at this stage that a client will need to be professionally advised. There are considerations that those involved in business may not take into account at such times so rushing a deal or paying insufficient attention to detail could have dire consequences.

Some clauses in what appear to be long-winded agreements may be given only a cursory glance, yet if something goes pear-shaped months or years after the conclusion of the contract these clauses could come back and bite if not given due attention.

Most commercial contracts are standard or have become a template from numerous past transactions of the law firm. So, to customise it to suit your particular circumstances each clause needs to be considered by you and your solicitor to determine whether it stays in or comes out. Insufficient attention to detail or rushing the solicitors to close negotiations could result in a clause or clauses unfavourable to you remaining in the contract.

One of the pitfalls of not paying sufficient attention to the inclusion or exclusion of clauses or understanding them is where two clauses conflict, thus giving an ambiguity on their meaning or interpretation.

This could result in a disadvantage to you in the future as once the contracts are signed, that's it, deal closed.

Tedious as wading through contract clauses line by line is, it advisable that you do this. If there is any language you do not understand ask your solicitor and be sure you are clear on its meaning. Unfortunately, most of these standard contracts are written in uncommonly used English and with legal jargon. There has been much discussion on removing the legal jargon from such contracts, but they are still there and that means we must deal with them.

Here a solicitor's previous experience in such contracts is vitally important. It is no use to you if you ask your solicitor the meaning of a sentence or clause and there is a delay in their response, or you get an *'I think ....'* A delay in their response could mean they are figuring out what it could mean. That is not good enough. For commercial contracts, be sure your solicitor has experience in this area.

These negotiations are often dealt with solicitor to solicitor and by mail or email exchange. This means the original agreement goes through several versions and it can become very tiresome seeing the same contract with marginal changes from version to version. But it must be done and giving clear instructions to your solicitor here will pay its way in spades.

Do

- Pay attention to detail.
- Ask questions if you are uncertain of a clause's interpretation.

Don't

- Don't skim over versions of the contract expecting 'others' to notice errors.

Chapter 8
Fees

The subject of fees has been touched on earlier but, as it is so important, it necessitates a closer look.

Fees can become a complicated issue if there is a lack of clarity on them and the client ends up with a legal bill that takes them by surprise. Solicitors want to ensure they get paid for their work so will broach the subject themselves at the initial meeting.

The solicitor charges for costs incurred in official forms by for example issuing summons and affidavits, but their main fee is for their time, i.e., their expertise.

Some legal services provided by the solicitor may have a standard charge rate, such as for wills or divorce, with a rider for complex matters; or you may agree to a fixed rate for the work to be done. Here the solicitor will know from experience how long the matter will take and can set a fixed fee.

Larger firms will charge by an hourly rate. For firms doing this you need to know the structure of how this works. For example, some firms may charge by the hour with fee time broken into units of four quarters. Here, whether a solicitor is speaking to the client for five minutes or fifteen minutes it is billed as one-quarter of the hourly rate. Alternatively, they may bill just the amount of time the conversation actually was, so five minutes would be billed as one-twelfth of the hourly (i.e. 60 minutes) rate. This is information you need to ascertain from the outset.

Hourly rates will differ significantly among law firms and there will be a difference in rates between the larger city firms and provincial firms.

Within the firms' rates, they will differ too between partners, junior solicitors, trainees, and paralegals. When discussing fees, find out whether additional solicitors/staff will be working on your case and their rates. Check too if trainees will be involved and whether you will be charged for their time and at what rate. Most law firms' websites will not give information on their fees so the only way of learning this is to ask the question.

In addition to the above, there are the extra costs known as 'outlay.' This is where you will be billed for photocopying, couriers, phone calls, scanning, stamps, etc. You need to ask what the firm's policy on this is. There is, I believe, a case to be made that such outlay should be part of the firm's overhead, and the client is not billed for them. Take for instance a situation where a solicitor has an hour-long telephone conversation with the client or on the business of the client with a third party, for which the client will be billed an hour's fee time. But will the client also be charged for the price of the phone call?

As mentioned in a previous chapter, you should give the solicitor all documents related to the legal matter you need their assistance on in good order to minimise the cost. Equally, you should only phone or communicate with the solicitor when you have something important to discuss. Prior to any such calls, make a list of the matters to be covered. Also, time and date the phone calls so you can check this when presented with your bill. A disorganised client who sends in bits of information and rings up their solicitor on minor matters will chalk up much bigger fees than they need to. The solicitor cannot be blamed for this. Most good solicitors are busy, and they too do not want to be wasting their time on unnecessary phone calls. So, use your solicitor's time wisely.

Some law firms will provide a 'no foal, no fee' (also known as 'no win, no fee') service in certain kinds of cases, but they need to be very confident of success before taking on the case. Also, in such instances, you need to learn what exactly you are getting free. In this instance, paying the outlay the solicitor will incur in taking on your case would be reasonable. This kind of service is more common in personal cases like personal injury than corporate work.

If going this route, you need to find out everything involved in the service they are doing for you.

Some law firms may offer a fixed fee rate for other kinds of work; this gives the client comfort in knowing what they are paying for. However, it would be unlikely this arrangement would apply to litigation, where the unpredictable can add considerable time and cost to a case.

When receiving invoices from your solicitor for services performed, you should request a full breakdown of fees and any other costs with a breakdown of items.

If an external lawyer is brought into a case, this will be a barrister. Your solicitor will first discuss it with you and give the reasons. You will be briefed on the need for a barrister and an estimate of their fee. Your solicitor will have to have your prior consent before bringing in a barrister.

There shouldn't be a mystery as to legal costs and the client should get a bill in line with expectations. This can only be achieved by dealing with the issue at an early stage of engagement.

Do

- Enquire about the system of fee calculation.
- Enquire about additional charges such as outlay.
- Seek itemised invoices.
- Make sure you fully understand everything discussed at the meeting and always ask questions.

Don't

- Don't waste your solicitor's time; this will simply add to your costs.
- Don't judge a solicitor on fees alone.
- Don't be unclear on fee issues.

Chapter 9
Understanding the Courts System

As a client of a solicitor, you need to understand how the system of litigation works. Once litigation is initiated the process is controlled by the courts system. It is generally thought that the litigation process is slow. Some believe the system of court vacations contribute to delays. However, the opposite is the case. The system needs breaks to catch up with the paperwork created by the system. Court registrars are sitting in court during hearings, but they have non-court work too and need time to get through it.

Judges of the higher courts have a huge workload. Often cases run into days or weeks and longer. They deliver oral judgments to some cases they hear on the day. These are at the conclusion of the case and delivered orally (known as *ex tempore*). But in longer cases they cannot deliver a judgment on the day with so much evidence to digest and consider and submitted cases law to be checked and considered so they need the vacation periods to consider the evidence and write up their judgments. On the day or evening preceding a new case they will read the court papers, so they have an idea of what the dispute is before the case opens. The Higher Court judges deliver multiple written judgments a year (known as reserved judgments).

The courts deal with different levels of damages so discuss with your solicitor which court your case falls within (see **Appendix 2**). This is very important as cases are heard much quicker in the Circuit Court than the High Court. If the amount of damages or compensation you are looking for is borderline on the €75,000 ceiling of the Circuit Court, to get the case dealt with sooner, it might be better to go for the Circuit Court and avoid long delays in the High Court.

Litigants can understandably become frustrated with delays waiting to get a hearing date due to the congestion of the lists. So, it makes sense at the outset to consider whether one of the forms of alternative dispute resolution (ADR) could resolve the disputed matter outside of the courts (see **Chapter 13**).

Nowadays there is a greater choice for resolving disputes; ADR or mediation can be used for a vast range of cases and can deal with the issues in a time limit where the restraints of our courts system do not get in the way.

Do

• Be patient and allow the system to take its course.

Don't

• Don't dismiss the option to use ADR or mediation or go to one of the specialist legal bodies without due consideration.

Chapter 10
Preparing for Court Hearings

Careful preparatory work which has taken months, even years, goes into being ready for your case to be heard in court. Getting documentation and witnesses ready for court is only part of the preparation; getting yourself ready is hugely important. It cannot be overstated how important it is for your head to be clear, your mind focused and you to be ready for this important day. Your solicitor will prepare you for:

• Delays in hearing dates, postponements and hanging around the court area waiting for your case to be called.
• Concern over raising costs.
• Feeling control slipping away from you.
• Concern about giving your own evidence.

A good solicitor will ease these pressures and go through how you will give evidence and respond to cross-examination. Remember court work is routine for litigation solicitors. Often the solicitor will be in constant contact with the client, to update them on progress – maybe settlement talks are happening (see more in **Chapter 13**) and generally put the client at ease the best they can in the strange clinical surroundings of the courthouse, while keeping an eye on the lists or being engaged in settlement talks with the other side.

This is the time to keep your nerve. Listen to the advice of your legal team.

Your solicitor will tell you when the date is listed for hearing. On that day you case will be listed in the Legal Diary. Here you will see where on the list your case is. If it's near the top you have a very good chance of your case being heard that day. But it is not uncommon that the judge may not get through the full list and so you have to come back another day.

Normally the list is read over to determine what cases are not 'going ahead' that day. Of the cases that remain, the judge will ask the solicitors or barristers how long they estimate their cases will last. This helps the judge to organise the list to enable as many cases as possible be heard.

While other cases ahead of yours on the list are being heard, all you can do is wait either in the court or outside it until your case is called. This can be boring and frustrating and get the nerves going. But remember, the other side will be experiencing exactly the same.

 If the waiting and the atmosphere of the court area gets to you, you could feel pressure to cave into a settlement. Remember the other side is going through the same pressures; listen to your solicitor and let the professionals act in your best interest.

For those who have never been in a court before, it would be helpful if you visit the court a week or so ahead of your court date. Here you will see how a court operates and might feel more at ease for your day in court.

Cross-examination

This is the hardest part of being a witness in your own case.

Your solicitor will advise you on giving evidence when he/she calls you to the stand and you can expect the questions as you will have discussed this in pre-court consultations. But when you finish your evidence, the solicitor or barrister for the other side will try and undermine your evidence.

It might seem they are twisting what you said in direct evidence. They will be seeking to trip you up. So be very careful in your answers to questions. Do not answer quickly, think about how they phrase the question. Do not volunteer any evidence, stick only to the question asked. Don't be afraid to ask for the question to be repeated or if you don't understand the question, say so.

Do

- Listen to the advice of your legal team at this crucial stage.
- Prepare yourself for court: get to the court in good time; dress respectfully – impressions count with judges.

Don't

- Don't have a late night before your court day, or drink excessive alcohol or have taken drugs.
- Don't throw away months of careful preparation by making rash decisions under pressure.
- In cross-examination, do not answer quickly, think about the question before answering and do not volunteer any additional information.

Chapter 11
Negotiations during Litigation

Whether you engage a solicitor for litigation or choose ADR (see **Chapter 13**), your solicitor will be involved in negotiations at some level. If you are purchasing or disposing of an asset or a service, the agreement that seals the deal will need to be put down on paper. Here your solicitor will be seeking the best terms for you and explaining what obligations, if any, arise under the agreement. This can be tedious work and requires the mind to be objective and focused on achieving the end goal.

Negotiation is the art of persuasion. It is important to discuss with your solicitor in advance the approach they will take in these negotiations, otherwise, it could result in an untimely intervention by you during the negotiations, which could undermine the point your solicitor was seeking to make. You need to act as a team.

A well-experienced negotiator will be in control of the talks and in observing their counterpart will employ subtle methods to win over the opposition to their way of thinking.

In negotiations it is interesting to see who is leading the way: are they being too pushy, are they being listened to or resisted by the opposing party? The solicitors do the talking but you, the client, should observe the personalities unwind, take notes, and then at an interval discuss with your solicitor what you are seeing. Often the solicitors will discuss between themselves and revert back to the client to tell them this position or take instructions.

There are different techniques in negotiation. A solicitor or barrister may at the outset try to develop a rapport with the other side through trivial conversation. If the solicitors know each other already the rapport is already there and could be more conducive to reaching a resolution faster than had they not known each other.

You should agree with your legal team in advance what concessions you are prepared to make in the negotiations. Your solicitor will be aware of these during the talks but will only introduce them or one of them when they believe that by doing so, they can get the other side to make a concession. They may hold back until there is a particular concession, they want the other party to make so they will bide their time. Their concession therefore becomes an inducement to the other side to concede on their point. Your solicitor in effect is luring their prey into their web.

Another technique would be for your solicitor to seek a substantial concession, knowing it is a big ask and will be declined. On being declined, they then make a more modest request. The object here is to make the other party feel good that your solicitor is willing to climb down on their initial request and hence make the other side more inclined to concede to the lesser request.

As the client, you need to understand the approaches your solicitor is making, or you risk putting your foot in it by saying something that could undermine your solicitor's well-thought-out plan of negotiation.

It is important to know in advance who the negotiators on the other side are. There is always a possibility that a senior solicitor may be on their team. This must be thought through. You do not want one party taking a dominant role because they are considered a person of authority. So, asserting one's position at an early stage in a subtle way could send out the signal to that senior person that they are not controlling the talks.

Skilled negotiators will see through the tricks of negotiation employed by the other party. As the client you should remain quiet and leave matters with your solicitor. You might feel intimidated and worried if the other party offers some concession but adds that there is only a limited time to accept. Your solicitor will understand the nuances of what is happening and play their hand when ready.

The lesson here is to be prepared, do your homework, work out the strategy with your solicitor in advance and trust them to deliver the best result for you.

Do

- Leave negotiations in the control of the professionals.
- Ensure you understand the approach taken.
- Ask questions if you are unsure of anything at this important stage.

Don't

- Don't undermine the work of your legal advisors.

Chapter 12
Settling Cases

When the possibility of settling your case arises, your solicitor will assess the issues and offer practical advice for you to consider. You can then instruct them accordingly. The solicitor will evaluate the risks and from experience give educated guesses on what the likely outcome may be.

All cases have risk, even very strong cases. If the other side know this and realise they have a weak case, the solicitor representing them, while knowing the limitations of their case, will nonetheless act as though they have a good case. So, like a game of poker, there is bluffing and gamesmanship going on and the solicitors know how to play this game. The clients sometimes lose their nerve as the court day nears but their solicitor does not and is there to fight your corner.

As the court day looms, settlement comes into the frame. It is not unusual for the parties' lawyers to have an 'off the record' conversation to sound out the other side. The solicitor with the weaker case may be looking for a way to settle the case and reduce the exposure of their client. On the other side, the stronger party may be interested in hearing what the other party has to say and see if an acceptable settlement can be reached which their client would be happy with. No settlement would be made without the client's agreement.

The party with the weaker case can save on cost exposure by settling the case and avoiding a full hearing with all the costs involved in that. This way the strong party could agree a settlement without having to give away too much and avoid the risk of something going wrong in court.

Settlement negotiations are a skill. Barristers excel as the courtroom is their workplace. The barrister is normally engaged in the higher courts (Circuit, High Court, Court of Appeal and Supreme Court).

During these settlement exchanges the solicitor is constantly weighing up the risks, the advantages, and the weak points, and evaluating whether, with the changing circumstances, they can get a settlement they can take back to you. The solicitor may come back to you and say the other side is offering X and they may add that they believe they can do better, so they advise you to decline. When that point arrives, conflicting thoughts will go through your head. You may be relieved and desire avoiding the hearing (hanging around a court can be unnerving) but try to remember the issues – do you believe you have a good case – and decide on the facts and issues of the case and not on how you feel on the day.

In settlement negotiations the lawyers are having a mini-run-through of the case in their exchanges, putting forward their strong points, and responding to points made by the other side. Always one party is more eager to settle than the other, but they won't let their guard down and will continue to push for their client even though they know they are on weak ground. The skill of settlement negotiation is critical. Your legal team is earning their fee here. Negotiation skills are honed by experience, so it is the home territory of the litigation practitioner.

Before a case gets near a court hearing lawyers representing opposing parties to a case may speak and a resolution could emerge from that; as the court date approaches, if neither party has shown a willingness to settle it is best to leave any settlement negotiations to the experts and see if anything emerges before the court date. Cases are often settled on the day of the hearing or just before the case starts.

If you and your legal team believe you have a good case it may be better to await your case. You need to be strong and not be intimidated by any claims by the opposing side. Keep your distance from the other side. Avoid contact if possible and let the lawyers meet away from you. If you are near the other side, in a corridor or tea-room for example, avoid direct contact, referring them to the lawyers who are managing the matter. If such contact is made, tell your solicitor.

In these situations, the trust you will have built up with your solicitor in the time leading up to the case is vitally important. You must have 100% confidence in your legal team.

Settlement talks can take time; if they are on the day of the court hearing and the time has come to start the case, a judge will often give the parties more time if they believe a settlement can be achieved.

In a negotiated settlement, you need to approach the process with a willingness to concede on some points. Your solicitor will advise on what these may be and what might appeal to the other party to achieve a settlement.

Do

- Trust your legal team in settlement matters.
- Be prepared to compromise.
- Listen to the advice of your legal team.

Don't

- Don't contact the other side without the knowledge of your legal team.
- Don't ignore the advice of your legal team.

Chapter 13
Alternative Dispute Resolution

Alternative dispute resolution, commonly referred to as ADR, has grown in popularity as a means of resolving disputes between parties. It involves training, which many solicitors now have, in techniques for disagreeing parties to come to an agreement that avoids litigation. It is, therefore, an alternative to the traditional route of resorting to the courts.

This form of redress can be used from simple disputes to more complex commercial cases. The procedure is there so it is clearly an alternative worthy of consideration for commercial disputes. ADR is an umbrella term that encompasses a number of different forms of non-litigious dispute resolution. Two of the most common forms of ADR are arbitration and mediation.

In arbitration a neutral third party, known as an 'arbitrator', imposes a legally binding resolution on the parties involved. Although parties may appeal arbitration outcomes to the court, such appeals face an exacting standard of review. In mediation, the neutral third party, known as a 'mediator', facilitates the resolution process (and may even suggest a resolution, typically known as a 'mediator's proposal') but does not impose a resolution on the parties. The terms of the agreement are decided upon by the parties involved. Generally, decisions made in mediation are not legally binding, unless both parties agree to it.

Arbitration, especially, has always been available for many years but I think there was a preference even among solicitors to take the litigation route rather than arbitration. But, that thinking has changed radically in recent years, and you only have to look at law firms' websites to see ADR is often offered as part of their services. An increasing number of solicitors, and indeed other professionals too, are trained in ADR. ADR has gained widespread acceptance among both the general public and the legal profession so a solicitor will not be annoyed if you suggest taking this route as a possibility. Your solicitor might raise it first as an option to resolve your problem.

The ADR procedure is more 'friendly' too than the austere surroundings of a courtroom. Litigation solicitors are comfortable in the latter as it is where they work, but litigants can often find the courts intimidating and unnerving. This obviously can have an impact on how they give evidence and could affect the outcome of a case. Think about it. You have spent months, even years, in painstakingly putting your case together and then your day in court arrives. You are out of your comfort zone in the courtroom, in surroundings unfamiliar to you. The legal practitioners and judge's language is foreign to you. You have a long wait for your case to come up: that wait could be days. The solicitors follow the practice and procedure of the system – a puzzle to the layman. There are last minute changes. Unless you are from another planet this must unsettle you in some way.

The ADR process is miles away from the litigation process. The third-party arbitrator or mediator is chosen by the parties. The hearing days are agreed and are not confined by any rules or vacation periods. Sitting times are like office hours. It's all very business-like, which allows the parties to relax in a way that is not possible in courtroom litigation. If the parties agree, the hearing could be on a weekend.

Litigation through the courts system is slow and one of the contributing reasons for that is the number of cases listed before the courts. ADR can reduce the pressure on the court system while benefiting both litigant and defendant through reduced costs, giving them control over who is the adjudicating party, an informal setting and greater privacy due to the confidentiality of the process.

There is a move that in some proceedings the courts now require parties to try mediation, and only if that fails do they allow the parties' case to be heard in court.

In taking a case to a solicitor, litigation may be in your mind but there are other options than just the litigation route. Most litigation cases are settled so it is worth exploring arbitration or mediation before issuing proceedings. Clients have more control over or input into the final resolution in mediation than through litigation. Arbitration is similar to litigation except it is done in private and in a more informal atmosphere. It is also faster than litigation as when your case is heard is not dictated by law terms or where your case is 'in the list'. But now there is a growing trend to mediation.

In arbitration you can still have your solicitor representing you so the process is quite similar to court litigation but there are procedural differences. You can agree with the other side who the arbitrator will be, whereas there is no such control in the court system. Papers are exchanged between the parties as in the litigation proceeding but the procedure is agreed by the parties. The parties can send in written submissions and the arbitrator makes their ruling without meeting the parties. Or there can be a hearing with evidence taken.

The ruling of the arbitrator is binding on both parties and consequently enforceable; there are some narrow exceptions to this but generally once you embrace the arbitration route the decision will have the same impact as that of a judge. In mediation, the parties themselves come to an agreed resolution. The decision is not legally enforceable unless the parties agree to make it so.

In relation to costs in arbitration, a typical order with regard to costs would follow what happens in the courts. However, an arbitrator has considerable discretion with regard to how he or she might award costs.

Your solicitor can advise whether they think an alternative to court litigation is best for your case and this should be raised at the initial meeting as an option.

Arbitration and mediation are growing in popularity and most law firms are engaging in these processes. They are certainly worth exploring to see if they benefit your problem.

Do

- Understand the differences between ADR and litigation before proceeding.
- Carefully consider whether arbitration or mediation would be the better option in your specific circumstances.

Don't

- Don't dismiss alternative options without considering them.
- Don't rush; weigh up which approach is best for you.

Chapter 14

What to Do if the Relationship with Your Solicitor Breaks Down

If you find your relationship with your solicitor runs into difficulty, the best course of action is to try to resolve it between yourself and the solicitor. The solicitor's firm may have a system in place to assist on such disputes, so explore this option.

Try to identify the cause of the breakdown. If you kept a file on progress, meetings, documents, calls, etc. you can trace the history of your working relationship with your solicitor and use this to your advantage. The best resolution is to work out a deal so the relationship can continue. Starting with a new law firm after the process has begun has its complications: finding a replacement solicitor; breaking them in and vice versa; agreeing fees; and placing your trust in a new solicitor. If the dispute involves fees, then the information given in **Chapter 8** comes to the fore. If you have not nailed down an agreement on fees at an early stage and a dispute arises over them it can become a mess. The Solicitors Regulatory Authority (SRA) is the body for complaints against registered solicitors. But this should be a last resort, try and resolves it with the solicitor first.

If you change your solicitor and your previous solicitor is owed fees, then he may not hand over the file to the new solicitor until his fee is paid. In effect, he has a lien on client files for his fees.

If proceedings have been issued, your previous solicitor must apply to the court to come off record.

So, changing solicitors is not straightforward hence the advice in spending time on choosing your solicitor in the first place and trying to resolve any problems before changing solicitors.

The Legal Services Regulatory Authority can investigate complaints against its members by clients on:
• Inadequate professional services.
• Excessive fees (there may be a time limit for such complaints).
• Misconduct.
• Breach of confidentiality.
• Failing to adhere to proper professional standards.
• Acting contrary to instructions.
• Being the cause of unjustified delays.
• Losing or destroying important documents.
• Bullying or coercion.

Full information can be found on the Legal Services Regulatory Authority website: **www.lsra.ie.**

Every effort should be made to resolve the subject matter of your complaint to avoid further delay, cost, and stress, and only if that fails should you take your complaint to the LSRA.

Do

• Talk to your solicitor to resolve the problem.
• Identify the cause of the breakdown.

Don't

• Don't get into a stand-off situation.
• Don't do nothing.

Appendix 1
The Barrister's Role

The legal profession in Ireland is divided into two branches: solicitors and barristers. The solicitor is the public's first contact for their legal problem. If the problem is neither complex nor involving the higher courts, then the solicitor can manage the matter, and it goes no further. But if it is a matter where special expertise is required or which normally involves the higher courts, namely, Circuit Court, High Court, Court of Appeal, and the Supreme Court. Your solicitor will tell you if your case requires a barrister (often referred to as counsel).

Strictly, the client of the barrister is the instructing solicitor, but in effect, they are acting for the client with the legal problem.

The barrister's fees are discharged by the solicitor on behalf of their client, so all financial matters are conducted between the client and the solicitor. While barristers engage in advisory work they are mainly employed in litigation.

Barristers operate essentially from the Law Library, Dublin 7. Some have offices in the surrounding area. The barristers are all self-employed and remain so throughout their careers.

While barristers engage in advisory work they are mainly employed in litigation.

Barristers are experts in presenting and arguing cases in court or tribunals. They are self-employed and under the system a solicitor can access the leading barristers in the country for a client, thereby enabling a small law firm, who may have a case against one of the biggest law firms in the country, to engage a top barrister to even out the playing field.

Barristers draft the court proceedings, prepare legal submissions in writing, and present the client's case in court. The solicitor will have gathered the information from the client and prepares a 'brief' for the barrister. The brief sets out the client's case with copies of relevant correspondence. The barrister devises a course of action from the brief and advises the solicitor. They in turn advise the client. In some instances, the barrister will advise there is no case and it would be a waste of money to pursue any action. Here the case ends, and the client is informed by their solicitor. In other cases, it may require the barrister to meet the client for a consultation to ascertain further information. Otherwise, the barrister may feel there is a case to answer and advise accordingly.

Courtroom skills of advocacy are central to a barrister's training. Documentary evidence for court proceedings can be required in evidence but often a case will be won or lost by the oral evidence of witnesses. Here the barrister's skill is best served. A well-argued case can be influential in persuading a judge (or jury) in your favour. Cross-examination of witnesses by your barrister could destroy or damage their case.

Barristers with specialist skills in court are in an advantageous position to advise on the strengths and weaknesses of their client's case and whether to fight the case or settle it through negotiations. Many of the cases coming before the courts are settled and it is the barrister who can advise you as to the best form of settlement and do the negotiations on your behalf.

Increasingly, barristers are engaged outside the traditional courtroom setting such as in mediations, arbitrations, tribunals, and disciplinary hearings.

Barristers are obliged by their professional body (the Bar Council) to give a written estimate of fees prior to undertaking work unless this is impossible due to the urgency of the matter, or the work is undertaken under the Civil Legal Aid Scheme.

Obtaining such an estimate will allow you and your solicitor to shop around to ensure that you obtain the best representation in terms of quality and price. Furthermore, the barrister must update the fee estimate as necessary if circumstances change. Solicitors often have a list of barristers whom they extensively use and with whom they have a good working relationship. However, for cases with a particular specialty, solicitors will go outside this list. If a client wants to use a specific barrister that is often agreed to by the solicitor provided, they are happy the barrister in question has, in the solicitor's opinion, the experience to deal with the matter.

There is no set scale of fees charged by barristers and the fee is usually negotiated by the solicitor on the client's behalf. The level of any particular fee must be based upon the work done having regard to the factors mentioned above. Like any profession, the most successful barristers, who are extremely busy, will charge more. The fee is for their time and expertise; there are no extras such as outlay or travel expenses.

The barrister profession has a tradition of ensuring that no one is left without proper representation simply because of their means. In these circumstances they provide services at less than the normal commercial rate or at no cost to the client. In appropriate cases which are not covered by legal aid schemes a barrister may be willing to take on a case on a 'no foal, no fee' basis. This means that the barrister will not require the payment of fees unless the client is successful (in which case the fees are usually ordered by the court to be paid by the other side).

Barristers are either junior or senior counsel. When a barrister commences practice, they are 'junior counsel.' A barrister can remain a junior counsel throughout their career or, after ten years or more, they can apply to become a Senior Counsel, sometimes referred to as a 'silk.' It is a position reserved for barristers of particular ability and experience. Judicial appointments are usually from the barrister ranks but an increasing number of appointments to the bench are solicitors.

When a solicitor engages a barrister, they normally bring in a junior counsel. If, in the opinion of the junior counsel, a Senior Counsel is required the solicitor will be informed. As this has a cost exposure the client will be consulted before a decision is made. In very complex cases more than one senior counsel may be advised to be brought onto a case.

A client may feel they don't need the addition of counsel, preferring the solicitor to represent them from beginning to end. This is of course possible. There will be a considerable workload on the solicitor who takes on the dual role of solicitor and the advocacy role of barrister. The courtroom is the workplace of the barrister, and they are best placed to speak on behalf of the client there. Also, there is the possibility of settlement, and this will require good negotiation skills to bring about the best result for the client. Some solicitors would feel up to the challenge, but it is a big ask, especially if on the other side there is a team of solicitors and barristers.

The work division of senior and junior barristers is that the senior counsel will do most of the advocacy work while the junior will take instructions from the senior and conduct research, case preparation and legal submissions, which are approved by the senior. However, in less complex cases or where the junior counsel is very experienced, they will share the advocacy workload.

Do

- Do trust the judgment of your solicitor if they believe the engagement of a barrister is necessary.
- Do trust the barrister in the same way as your solicitor, they have been specifically chosen by your solicitor for this matter.

Don't

- Don't take the risk of going without a barrister if your solicitor recommends it.
- Don't distance yourself from the engagement of a barrister; they are an addition to your team.

Appendix 2
The Courts

The Supreme Court

The Supreme Court is the highest court in Ireland. It hears appeals from the Court of Appeal and the High Court in the limited circumstances set out in the Constitution.

Under Article 26 of the Irish Constitution, the President of Ireland may refer any Bill passed by the Oireachtas to the Supreme Court to decide whether it is unconstitutional.

The Supreme Court of Ireland sits at the top of the Irish courts system and is the court of final appeal in civil and criminal matters. It also has the final say in respect of the interpretation of Ireland's basic law, *Bunreacht na hÉireann* (the Constitution of Ireland). As the highest court in the land, the decisions of the Supreme Court are binding on all other courts in Ireland.

1. General Appellate Jurisdiction
Appeals are only heard where the Supreme Court grants permission once it determines that the relevant test set out in Article 34.5 of the Constitution has been satisfied.

Constitutional Tests
The Supreme Court hears appeals from decisions of the **Court of Appeal** where it is satisfied:

• that the decision involves a matter of general public importance, or
• in the interests of justice, it is necessary that there be an appeal to the Supreme Court.

The Supreme Court can also hear appeals from decisions of the **High Court** where it is satisfied that there are exceptional circumstances warranting a direct appeal to it, a precondition for the Court being so satisfied is the presence of either or both of the following factors:

• The decision involves a matter of general public importance, and/or
• It is in the interests of justice.

This is commonly referred to as a 'leapfrog' appeal because it bypasses the Court of Appeal.

2. Constitutional Jurisdiction
The Supreme Court has the final say in the interpretation of the Constitution of Ireland. It ensures that the laws enacted by the Oireachtas, Ireland's Parliament, are upheld and interpreted in light of the Constitution and the jurisprudence that has developed since it came into force in 1937. In that way, it may be said to function as a constitutional court.

This is a role of particular importance in Ireland as the Constitution expressly permits the courts to review any law, whether passed before or after the enactment of the Constitution, in order to determine whether it conforms with the Constitution. The Superior Courts (the High Court, Court of Appeal and Supreme Court) retain the power to declare invalid legislation that is determined to be inconsistent with the Constitution.

3. Original Jurisdiction
The Supreme Court has original jurisdiction to deal with two particular matters when called on:

• Where a bill is referred to the Supreme Court by the President of Ireland, in accordance with Article 26 of the Constitution, for a determination of whether that bill (or certain provisions of it), as passed by both Houses of the Oireachtas, is incompatible with the Constitution, and
• Where the Supreme Court has been requested to determine, in accordance with Article 12.3 of the Constitution, whether the President of Ireland is incapacitated.

To date, no requests under Article 12.3 have come before the Supreme Court.

Article 26 Procedure

- Where the decision to refer a bill to the Supreme Court is made by the President, a constitutionally prescribed time limit of 60 days commences. During this time the Supreme Court must assign counsel to argue the unconstitutionality of the bill, hear oral arguments, adjudicate on the matter, and give its decision. The Government's chief legal advisor, the Attorney General, argues in favour of the bill's constitutionality.
- The decision reached by the Supreme Court in an Article 26 reference is required by the Constitution to be delivered in the form of a single judgment, where only the decision of the majority of the Court is given.
- Where the Court decides that a bill is incompatible with the Constitution, that bill must not be signed into law by the President.
- Where the constitutionality of the bill is upheld by the Court, the bill is signed into law by the President and afforded indefinite immunity from further constitutional challenge.

Since the enactment of the Constitution in 1937, the Article 26 mechanism has been invoked by the President of the day on 16 occasions, with the Supreme Court determining in seven of those cases that the bill was incompatible with the Constitution.

4. Implementation of EU Law

Article 267 Preliminary Reference Procedure: The Supreme Court has a role in implementing the law of the European Union. As the court of final appeal in Ireland, it is obliged under the *Treaty on the Functioning of the European Union* to refer to the Court of Justice of the European Union questions regarding the interpretation of EU law which arise in cases before it, where the interpretation is not clear, and clarification is necessary in order for the Supreme Court to decide a question before it.

The Court of Appeal

The Court of Appeal hears appeals in civil cases from the High Court. It can also give rulings on questions of law raised in the Circuit Court.

Jurisdiction of the Court

As with the other Superior Courts, some of the jurisdiction of the Court of Appeal is conferred by the Constitution and some by legislation. The Court of Appeal has authority to hear the following appeals:

A- The Court has jurisdiction to hear appeals in civil proceedings from the High Court:
   (i) which prior to the Thirty-third Amendment of the Constitution would have been heard by the Supreme Court.
   (ii) The Court can hear appeals from cases heard in the High Court about whether or not a law is constitutional. The Constitution provides that no laws may be passed restricting the Court of Appeal's jurisdiction to do this.

B- Under the *Court of Appeal Act*, 2014, the Court of Appeal was given the 'appellate jurisdiction' previously exercised by the Court of Criminal Appeal.
   (i) Appeals by persons convicted on indictment in the Circuit Court, Central Criminal Court and Special Criminal Court now lie to the Court of Appeal. Appeals against the severity of a sentence imposed by those courts also lie to the Court of Appeal.
   (ii) The Court of Appeal was also given jurisdiction to hear appeals by the Director of Public Prosecutions on a question of law arising out of criminal trials which resulted in an acquittal.

C- Under the *Court of Appeal Act*, 2014, the Court of Appeal was given the appellate jurisdiction previously exercised by the Courts-Martial Appeal Court.
   (i) The appeal is determined on a record of the proceedings at the courts-martial with power to hear new or additional evidence or to refer any matter for report to the president or the judge advocate of the courts-martial.
   (ii) If the appeal is against the finding and the sentence, the court may affirm or reverse the finding in whole or in part or order a new trial or vary the sentence.
   (iii) If the appeal is limited to either finding or sentence, the court is confined to dealing with the matter which is the subject of the appeal.

(iv) The court also has power to review a finding or sentence (which was the subject of a previous appeal) where new evidence shows that there has been a miscarriage of justice.

Composition of the Court

The Court of Appeal is composed of a President and 15 ordinary judges. The Chief Justice and the President of the High Court are *ex officio* judges of the Court of Appeal.

The Court may sit in divisions of three judges. Some interlocutory and procedural applications may be heard by the President alone or by another judge nominated by the President.

Questions of law which could previously be referred by the Circuit Court to the Supreme Court for determination (a 'case stated') are now determinable by the Court of Appeal.

Appeals transferred from Supreme Court to Court of Appeal

Following the establishment of the Court of Appeal, specified appeals pending in the Supreme Court which had been initiated before the establishment day and had not been fully or partly heard by that court were directed by the Chief Justice to be heard and determined by the Court of Appeal.

The High Court

The High Court is based in Dublin and has the power to hear all criminal and civil matters (including family law cases) but usually hears only those cases that cannot be dealt with by the lower courts.

This means that, in civil actions, it hears cases where the claim exceeds €38,000.

It also hears appeals from the Circuit Court in civil matters and can give rulings on questions of law raised in the District Court.

The High Court has full jurisdiction to determine all matters on civil or criminal questions. This means that there is no limit on how much money can be awarded by the High Court in compensation or damages.

When the High Court is hearing criminal matters it is known as the Central Criminal Court. In criminal matters, the High Court Judge sits with a jury of 12 people.

Jurisdiction

The High Court has full jurisdiction in and power to determine all matters and questions whether of law or fact, civil or criminal. Its jurisdiction also extends to the question of the validity of any law having regard to the Constitution.

The High Court acts as an appeal court from the Circuit Court in civil matters. It has power to review the decisions of certain tribunals. It may also give rulings on questions of law submitted by the District Court.

A person granted bail in the District Court may apply to the High Court to vary the conditions of bail. If the District Court refuses bail, application may be made to the High Court. A person charged with murder can only apply to the High Court for bail.

In terms of the Central Criminal Court, the court sits at such time and in such places as the President of the High Court may direct and tries criminal cases which are outside the jurisdiction of the Circuit Court.

Composition of the High Court

The High Court consists of the President and 36 ordinary judges. The Chief Justice, the President of the Court of Appeal, and the President of the Circuit Court are, by virtue of their office, additional judges of the High Court.

Matters coming before the High Court are normally heard and determined by one judge, but the President of the High Court may decide that any cause or matter or any part thereof may be heard by three judges in what is known as a divisional court.

In terms of Criminal trials, they are conducted by a single judge sitting with a jury of 12 people, but the President of the High Court may direct two or more judges to sit together for the purpose of a particular trial.

Sittings

The High Court sits in Dublin to hear original actions. It also hears personal injury and fatal injury actions in several provincial locations (Cork, Galway, Limerick, Waterford, Sligo, Dundalk, Kilkenny and Ennis), at specified times during the year. In addition, the High Court sits in provincial venues to hear appeals from the Circuit Court in civil and family law matters.

The central criminal court mainly hears murder and rape trials and since the *Competition Act*, 2002, also criminal trials under that Act. Traditionally, the court sat exclusively in Dublin. In recent years the court has sat in Limerick, Sligo, Ennis, Cork and Castlebar.

Appeals

Appeals in civil proceedings from the High Court can be taken to the Court of Appeal, except for those cases in which the Supreme Court has permitted an appeal to it (a 'leap frog' appeal). This follows the establishment of the Court of Appeal on 28 October 2014.

An appeal against conviction or sentence by the Central Criminal Court may be taken to the Court of Appeal.

The Circuit Court

The Circuit Court is organised on a regional basis.

It deals with civil cases which do not exceed €75,000. It can also deal with some liquor licensing cases and a wide range of family law cases including divorce and judicial separation.

The Circuit Court also hears appeals from the District Court in civil and criminal matters.

The Circuit Court is a court of local and limited jurisdiction. It is restricted as to which cases it can decide in both civil and criminal matters.

The country is divided into 8 circuits for the purposes of the Circuit Court, which comprises the President of the Court and up to 45 ordinary judges. One Circuit Judge is assigned to each circuit, except in Dublin, where 10 judges may be assigned, and Cork, where there is provision for 3 judges.

Jurisdiction

The Circuit Court is a court of limited and local jurisdiction. The work can be divided into three main areas: civil, criminal and family law. Cork, Dublin and Limerick have continuous Circuit Court sittings throughout each legal term. In all other parts of the country, there is a calendar for Circuit Court sittings.

A- Civil Business

The civil jurisdiction of the Circuit Court is a limited one unless all parties to an action consent, in which event the jurisdiction is unlimited. The limit of the court's jurisdiction relates mainly to actions where the claim does not exceed €75,000 and the market value does not exceed €3,000,000.

B- Criminal

In criminal matters the Circuit Court has the same jurisdiction as the Central Criminal Court in all indictable offences except murder, rape, aggravated sexual assault, treason, piracy and related offences. This jurisdiction is exercisable in the area where the offence has been committed or where the accused person has been arrested or resides. However, in Circuit Courts outside Dublin, the trial judge may transfer a trial to the Dublin Circuit Criminal Court on application by the prosecution or the defence and if satisfied that it is not unjust to do so. Criminal cases dealt with by the Circuit Criminal Court begin in the District Court and are sent forward to the Circuit Court for trial or sentencing. Trials are conducted by a single judge sitting with a jury of 12 people.

C- Family Law

The Circuit and High Court have concurrent jurisdiction in the area of Family Law. The Circuit Court has authority in a wide range of family law proceedings: judicial separation, divorce, nullity and appeals from the District Court. In hearing such cases, the Circuit Court has authority to make related orders, including custody and access orders, maintenance and barring orders. Applications for protection and barring orders may also be made directly to the Circuit Court. Applications to dispense with the three months' notice period of marriage are also dealt with by the Circuit Court.

Composition
The country is divided into eight circuits with one judge assigned to each circuit except in Dublin where 10 judges may be assigned, and Cork, where there is provision for three judges.

Appeals from the District Court
Decisions of the District Court can be appealed to the Circuit Court with some exceptions. Appeals proceed by way of a full rehearing and the decision of the Circuit Court is final.

The Circuit Court also acts as an appeal court for appeals from the decisions of the Labour Court, Unfair Dismissals Tribunal and the Employment Appeals Tribunal.

The Circuit Court is divided in eight regions:

- Dublin Circuit (covering city and county).
- Cork Circuit (covering city and county).
- Eastern Circuit (covering Kildare, Meath Louth and Wicklow).
- Midland Circuit (covering Longford, Offaly, Roscommon, Sligo and Westmeath).
- Northern Circuit (covering Cavan, Donegal, Leitrim and Monaghan).
- South Eastern Circuit (covering Carlow, Kilkenny, Tipperary, Waterford and Wexford).
- South Western Circuit (covering Clare, Kerry and Limerick).
- Western Circuit (Covering Galway and Mayo).

The District Court

The District Court is organised on a local basis throughout the country. It deals with civil actions where compensation claimed does not exceed €15,000. Consumers can use the small claims procedure in the District Court to recover sums up to €2,000.

It also handles liquor licensing cases and a wide range of family law cases, including custody and maintenance of children and applications for barring orders.

The District Court also deals with criminal matters such as drunk driving, speeding, assault, criminal damage and the initial hearings of serious offences to be tried in the higher courts.

A judge sitting alone deals with these cases.

The District Court is a court of local and summary jurisdiction. The business of the District Court can be divided into four categories: criminal, civil, family law and licensing.

Civil Business
The civil jurisdiction of the District Court in contract and most other matters is where the claim or award does not exceed €15,000.

Criminal Business
The District Court exercising its criminal jurisdiction deals with four particular types of offences:

- Summary offences – these are offences for which there is no right of trial by judge and jury. This makes up the bulk of the criminal work of the District Court, these offences are exclusively statutory in origin.
- Indictable offences tried summarily – with the consent of the accused and the DPP and the judge being of the opinion that the facts constitute a minor offence.
- Indictable offences – other than certain offences including rape, aggravated sexual assault, murder, treason and piracy where the accused

pleads guilty and the DPP consents, and the judge accepts the guilty plea. Otherwise, the accused is sent forward to the Circuit Court on his signed plea of guilty for sentencing.
- Indictable offences not tried summarily. With regard to these offences, a Book of Evidence is served on the accused. The judge considers the Book of Evidence and any submissions on behalf of the defence or the prosecution. If the judge is of the opinion that there is a sufficient case to answer, the accused is sent forward to the Circuit Court or Central Criminal Court for trial.

Family Law
The District Court has a wide jurisdiction in the family law area. Proceedings are not heard in open court and are as informal as is practicable.

1. **Domestic violence:** Under the *Domestic Violence Act, 2018*, there are two main types of remedies – Safety Orders and Barring Orders.
2. **Guardianship of children:** Under the *Guardianship of Infants Act, 1964*, as amended by the *Status of Children's Act, 1987*, the District Court can make custody and access orders and appoint guardians. It also has jurisdiction to establish paternity in relation to any child, with regard to an application for custody, access or maintenance.
3. **Maintenance:** Under the *Maintenance of Spouses and Children Act, 1976* (as amended), the District Court can award maintenance to a spouse and child(ren). The maximum that can be awarded to a spouse is €500 per week and for a child €150 per week. To enforce the order the court can direct that all payments be paid through the District Court office, make attachment of earnings or issue a warrant for the arrest of the defaulting debtor.
4. **Child care:** Under the *Child Care Act, 1991*, the HSE can make a number of applications to court for orders.

Licensing
The District Court also has wide powers in relation to liquor and lottery licensing.

Miscellaneous

The District Court also deals with miscellaneous actions such as actions taken under the *Control of Dogs Acts*, applications for citizenship, applications to amend birth and marriage certificates and applications under the *Environmental Protection Act, 1992*, for orders in connection with noise reduction.

Composition

The country is divided into 23 districts with one or more judges permanently assigned to each district and the Dublin Metropolitan District.

Generally, the venue at which a case is heard depends on where an offence was committed. or where the defendant resides or carries on business, or was arrested. Each District Court office (with the exception of the Dublin Metropolitan District Court) deals with all elements of the work of the District Court. The District Court is known as a court of 'local and summary jurisdiction'.

Appeals

The District Court has a limited jurisdiction in respect of decisions made by statutory bodies and in these appeals, the decision of the District Court is final except where a point of law is at issue. In such instances an appeal can be taken to the High Court.

(Reproduced by kind permission of the Courts Services, more information at **www.courts.ie.**)

Appendix 3

Section 68 of the *Solicitors (Amendment) Act, 1994*

Charges to clients

68.—(1) On the taking of instructions to provide legal services to a client, or as soon as is practicable thereafter, a solicitor shall provide the client with particulars in writing of—

(a) the actual charges, or

(b) where the provision of particulars of the actual charges is not in the circumstances possible or practicable, an estimate (as near as may be) of the charges, or

(c) where the provision of particulars of the actual charges or an estimate of such charges is not in the circumstances possible or practicable, the basis on which the charges are to be made,

by that solicitor or his firm for the provision of such legal services and, where those legal services involve contentious business, with particulars in writing of the circumstances in which the client may be required to pay costs to any other party or parties and the circumstances, if any, in which the client's liability to meet the charges which will be made by the solicitor of that client for those services will not be fully discharged by the amount, if any, of the costs recovered in the contentious business from any other party or parties (or any insurers of such party or parties).

(2) A solicitor shall not act for a client in connection with any contentious business (not being in connection with proceedings seeking only to recover a debt or liquidated demand) on the basis that all or any part of the charges to the client are to be calculated as a specified percentage or proportion

of any damages or other moneys that may be or may become payable to the client, and any charges made in contravention of this subsection shall be unenforceable in any action taken against that client to recover such charges.

(3) A solicitor shall not deduct or appropriate any amount in respect of all or any part of his charges from the amount of any damages or other moneys that become payable to a client of that solicitor arising out of any contentious business carried out on behalf of that client by that solicitor.

(4) Subsection (3) of this section shall not operate to prevent a solicitor from agreeing with a client at any time that an amount on account of charges shall be paid to him out of any damages or other moneys that may be or may become payable to that client arising out of any contentious business carried out on behalf of that client by that solicitor or his firm.

(5) Any agreement under subsection (4) of this section shall not be enforceable against a client of a solicitor unless such agreement is in writing and includes an estimate (as near as may be) of what the solicitor reasonably believes might be recoverable from any other party or parties (or any insurers of such party or parties) in respect of that solicitor's charges in the event of that client recovering any damages or other moneys arising out of such contentious business.

(6) Notwithstanding any other legal provision to that effect a solicitor shall show on a bill of costs to be furnished to the client, as soon as practicable after the conclusion of any contentious business carried out by him on behalf of that client—

(a) a summary of the legal services provided to the client in connection with such contentious business,
(b) the total amount of damages or other moneys recovered by the client arising out of such contentious business, and
(c) details of all or any part of the charges which have been recovered by that solicitor on behalf of that client from any other party or parties (or any insurers of such party or parties),

and that bill of costs shall show separately the amounts in respect of fees, outlays, disbursements and expenses incurred or arising in connection with the provision of such legal services.

(7) Nothing in this section shall prevent any person from exercising any existing right in law to require a solicitor to submit a bill of costs for taxation, whether on a party and party basis or on a solicitor and own client basis, or shall limit the rights of any person or the Society under section 9 of this Act.

(8) Where a solicitor has issued a bill of costs to a client in respect of the provision of legal services and the client disputes the amount (or any part thereof) of that bill of costs, the solicitor shall—

    (a) take all appropriate steps to resolve the matter by agreement with the client, and

    (b) inform the client in writing of—

        (i) the client's right to require the solicitor to submit the bill of costs or any part thereof to a Taxing Master of the High Court for taxation on a solicitor and own client basis, and

        (ii) the client's right to make a complaint to the Society under section 9 of this Act that he has been issued with a bill of costs that he claims to be excessive.

(9) In this section "charges" includes fees, outlays, disbursements and expenses.

(10) The provisions of this section shall apply notwithstanding the provisions of the *Attorneys and Solicitors (Ireland) Act, 1849*, and the *Attorneys and Solicitors Act, 1870*.

Appendix 4
Key Legal Terms Explained

Abstract of title: A list of the documents and facts constituting the vendor's (seller's) title to land and certain interests in land prepared when land is sold.

Act of God: An occurrence that has its origin in the agency of natural forces – for example, an earthquake – that could prevent a contract or transaction taking place.

Agent: Someone who acts on behalf of someone else – for example, a conveyancer.

Aggravated damages: An increased amount of damages awarded by a court where the defendant's conduct was so reckless as to injure the plaintiff to an exceptional degree.

Anton Piller order: An order in civil proceedings allowing one party to enter another's party's property to inspect and remove documents and other items. It is normally granted to prevent an anticipated removal or destruction of possible evidence.

Assign: To formally transfer something.

Beneficial interest: An asset belonging to a person, even though someone else is the legal owner.

Beneficiary: Someone who is entitled to a benefit – for example, under a will or trust.

Bill of costs: The invoice a solicitor will send a client after work is finished, containing the solicitor's fee, expenses and disbursements.

Brief: The written instructions prepared by a solicitor for a barrister prior to the court hearing.

Caveat: A warning – for example, *caveat emptor*: a warning to a buyer: 'buyer beware'.

Certiorari: An order by the High Court that a case should be reviewed.

Concealment: Failure to disclose all information in a contract.

Copyright: The exclusive right to make copies of an original work.

Damages (exemplary): An amount of damages that is so great as to make an example of the defendant's wrongdoing.

Damages (general): Such damages as the court presumes to have resulted from a civil wrong.

Damages (punitive): An award of heavy damages to punish the defendant in a civil action whose conduct has been of a flagrant nature and a gross infringement of the plaintiff's right. The reason for this is that it is the function of the civil courts to compensate.

Damages (special): Direct loss and damage as the plaintiff can prove they suffered as a consequence of the defendant's wrongful conduct.

Defamation: The publication of words injurious to another person's good name and character or reputation. There are two kinds defamation: libel (the written word) and slander (the offending words spoken).

Ex parte: Proceedings conducted on behalf of one party to a civil action in the absence of the other party.

In camera: A court hearing in which the public is excluded from the court.

Indemnity: Compensation for – or protection against – loss or damages that might be given by one person to another within a contract or otherwise.

Injunction: A court order directing a party to do, or refrain from doing, something. An injunction can be ad interim (temporary), interlocutory (continuing) or perpetual (permanent). There are different kinds of injunctions, including Mareva Injunctions, which bars a defendant from removing their assets from the jurisdiction until the hearing of the case.

Intellectual property: Ideas you create and legally own as a result of owning a copyright, trademark or patent.

Interim proceedings: Hearings that take place between the first hearing and the final hearing.

Mandamus: A writ by the High Court ordering a lower court to perform some duty.

Money laundering: The process of concealing the source of illegally obtained money.

Paralegal: Someone who supports lawyers in their work. Often paralegals have a law degree but do not have a practicing qualification.

Pro bono: Professional work undertaken voluntarily and without payment or at a reduced fee.

Sub judice: A term used when legal proceedings have been commenced where public comment is forbidden and breach of this can amount to contempt of court.

Subpoena: A summons addressed to a witness compelling their attendance in court for the hearing of the action.

Tenancy: A contract between a tenant and their landlord. This contract can be written or verbal.

Third party: A term used to describe someone other than the two sides in a particular situation.

Ultra vires: Beyond the power of.

Without prejudice: A term used in relation to a letter written or an admission made during negotiations on the understanding that it will not be used against the party making it in the event of a court hearing.

Appendix 5
Useful Organisations

Bar Council of Ireland
Bar Council Administration Office
Distillery Building, 145-51 Church Street, Dublin 7
T: (01) 817 5000; E: thebarofireland@lawlibrary.ie; W: www.lawlibrary.ie

Courts Service
15-24 Phoenix Street North, Smithfield, Dublin 7
Tel: (01) 888 6000; W: www.courts.ie

Dublin Dispute Resolution Centre
Distillery Building, 145-51 Church Street, Dublin 7
T: (01) 817 5277; E: ddrc@lawlibrary.ie; W: www.dublinarbitration.ie

ISME (Irish Small & Medium Firms Association)
17 Kildare Street, Dublin 2
Tel: (01) 662 2755; E: info@isme.ie; W: www.isme.ie

Law Society of Ireland
Blackhall Place, Dublin 7
T: (01) 672 4800; F: (01) 6724801; E: general@lawsociety.ie;
W: www.lawsociety.ie

Legal Service Regulatory Authority (LSRA)
PO Box 12906, Dublin 7
T: (01) 859 2911; E: Isra-inbox@Isra.ie; W: www.Isra.ie

Mediators' Institute of Ireland
The Capel Building, Mary's Abbey, Dublin 7
T: (01) 609 9190; E: info@themii.ie; W: www.themii.ie

Small Firms Association

84-84 Lower Baggot Street, Dublin 2
Tel: (01) 605 1500; E: info@ibec.ie; W: www.ibec.ie/sfa